LIBRARY

00905 1793

W9-BCY-079

DEC 21 2000

Skerry, Brian

A whale on her
own

$ 18.95

DUE DATE

NANUET
PUBLIC
LIBRARY

A Whale On Her Own

The True Story of Wilma the Beluga Whale

Text and Photos by Brian Skerry

BLACKBIRCH PRESS, INC.

WOODBRIDGE, CONNECTICUT

NANUET PUBLIC LIBRARY

Published by Blackbirch Press, Inc.
260 Amity Road
Woodbridge, CT 06525

©2000 by Blackbirch Press, Inc.
First Edition

Distributed in Canada exclusively by VanWell Publishing
P.O. Box 2131, 1 Northrup Crescent
St. Catharines, Ontario L2R 7S2

e-mail: staff@blackbirch.com
Web site: www.blackbirch.com

All rights reserved. No part of this book may be reproduced in any form without permission in writing from Blackbirch Press, Inc., except by a reviewer.

Printed in China

10 9 8 7 6 5 4 3 2 1

Photo Credits

All images ©Brian Skerry, except page 3: ©Corel Corporation; and page 27 (left): ©PhotoDisc.

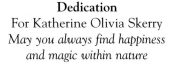

Dedication
For Katherine Olivia Skerry
*May you always find happiness
and magic within nature*

Library of Congress Cataloging-in-Publication Data

Skerry, Brian.
A Whale On Her Own: the true story of Wilma the beluga whale / text and photos by Brian Skerry.—1st ed.
    p.   cm.
Includes bibliographical references and index.
Summary: An orphaned white whale arrives in a small bay near Nova Scotia where it finds acceptance by the local community and friendship with a SCUBA diver until it suddenly disappears.
ISBN 1-56711-431-8
1. White whale—Nova Scotia—Chedabucto Bay—Biography—Juvenile literature.
2. Chedabucto Bay (N.S.). [1. White whale. 2. Whales.] I. Title.
QL737.C433 S54 2000
599.5'42'0929—dc21

99-054786
CIP
AC

Can you imagine what it would be like to swim with a whale? How would it feel to glide beneath the ocean waves with a graceful animal as your guide? It would be truly magical to explore the sea with a whale for a friend.

For such a thing to happen, though, a whale would have to want to be with you. But, is that even possible? Whales are wild animals. They almost never come face to face with humans.

Most whales spend their days searching for food. They hunt and swim together in groups called pods. Few wild whales will ever see or hear a human being.

Once in a while, however, the lives of humans and wild animals come together. These dream-like moments are truly gifts from nature. They make us believe that maybe all animals—including whales—can dream, too.

Some time ago, in a quiet little bay in Nova Scotia, Canada, a young beluga whale was seen swimming near the shore. She was first spotted by a group of fishermen on their way out to sea. They believed the whale was just passing through and would not stay. A few days later, she was seen again. This time, word of the beluga whale began to spread throughout the village.

Seeing a whale all by itself was rather strange. Beluga whales usually swim together in large groups. It was also unusual to see a beluga whale as far south as Nova Scotia. Belugas ordinarily live much farther north, in the Arctic.

Chedabucto Bay is a small, circle-shaped harbor. Glistening fishing boats lie anchored on its silky, smooth water. Surrounding the harbor are hills of thick green trees. Soaring through blue sky, osprey and eagles patrol the open water. From high above, they wait to swoop and dive at the first sight of a fish. These peaceful surroundings made Chedabucto Bay a welcome place for a wandering beluga whale to visit.

As time passed, people were surprised that the animal did not move on. Some believed that the whale's mother had died, leaving the young beluga an orphan. Not knowing how to return to her pod, she settled into Chedabucto Bay.

The young whale was most often seen near a large, red buoy that was anchored within the bay. The buoy helped boats find their way through the harbor. It always floated in exactly the same place. Its rusty anchor chain rattled and clanged as the waves moved it back and forth.

The lonely beluga appeared to find comfort in being near the red buoy. She seemed to enjoy the clang-clang-clanging of its hollow bell. Some people joked that she had "adopted" the buoy as her new mother.

After many months, locals thought of the whale as a member of their community. Someone named her Wilma. The name caught on quickly. Soon she was the most famous resident of Chedabucto Bay.

One person who became especially interested in Wilma was Jim Johnson. Jim had lived near Chedabucto Bay all of his life. He had also spent much of his time at sea in search of adventure. He had traveled around the world on great sailing ships and lived among seals in the frozen north. He had even searched for sunken treasure off the sandy shores of tropical islands!

Jim was an experienced SCUBA diver. He had seen many amazing animals underwater. And all throughout his life, he had dreamed of coming face to face with a beluga whale. When Jim heard that a beluga was now living in Chedabucto Bay, he could not believe it. One day, he decided to see for himself.

Jim loaded his diving gear into a small inflatable boat and sailed out into the open water. The morning sunlight reflected off the glassy surface as Jim glided toward a small rocky beach. He pulled his boat up on shore and put on his SCUBA gear.

Jim dipped beneath the water's surface, and swam down until he was about 20 feet deep. He was excited—he was not sure what to expect. He very much wanted to see Wilma, but he was sure she would never come close enough to him.

Silent and alone, Jim stared out into the bright, green water. He could not see very far in front of him. He could see the bay's rocky bottom, a few small fish, and some seashells. Other than that, Jim saw nothing. He knelt down on the bottom. A trickle of icy cold water ran down his neck. It sent a shiver through his body. He looked straight ahead one more time. Then, from out of nowhere, Wilma appeared before his eyes!

She swam slowly toward Jim at first. She moved in and out of his vision, like a watery ghost. The closer she got to him, the more real she became. She circled around and stopped right in front of him. Jim could not believe what he was seeing. He was only inches away from a wild beluga whale! Sunlight trickled through the water. It cast a glow on Wilma's soft, round body. She was stunning. A milky white whale floating in an emerald green sea.

Jim moved very slowly. Not wanting to frighten Wilma, he reached out his hand. The whale stared cautiously at the human. Then she moved toward him. Gently, she touched the top of her head to his palm. She pushed ever so slightly. Jim rubbed her head and ran his hand along the side of her body. Her skin felt smooth, cold, and rubbery. Wilma swam in slow circles around Jim, letting him stroke her back. Then she glided away into the sea, leaving him alone once again.

Jim's whole body was shaking from excitement. He had finally done it. He had made contact with a wild beluga whale. But, was that it? Was this brief meeting to be their only time together?

As weeks went by, Jim met Wilma nearly every day. The friendship between them grew quickly. Jim even invented a way of calling Wilma when he could not see her underwater. He knew that whales are able to "see" things underwater by using sounds called sonar. They bounce high-pitched sound waves off objects to tell them where things around them are located. Jim decided to use a similar technique. By banging two stones together underwater, he sent out a signal to Wilma. This sound told her exactly where he was. Usually, within a few minutes of using this "underwater telegraph," Wilma appeared.

Often, Jim and Wilma would swim together along the bottom of the bay. One day, Jim discovered that Wilma liked to swim upside down. He also noticed that she enjoyed rubbing her head on the bay's gravelly bottom.

Together, they explored the sea floor. And they discovered many beautiful things. Flat, round sand dollars carpeted the gray, sandy bottom. Shy lobsters and curious fish peeked out from beneath stony ridges. Colorful, orange anemones swayed in the gentle current.

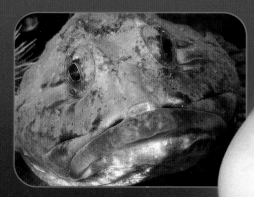

As they played, Wilma would swim to the surface every few minutes for a breath. (Like humans, whales are mammals that must breathe air.) Then she would re-join Jim on the bottom for more adventures.

While swimming with Jim, Wilma rarely dived any deeper than 30 feet. This is a shallow depth for a beluga. Some belugas can dive as deep as 3,000 feet in search of food. To do this, they have been known to hold their breath for up to 25 minutes!

When Jim was with Wilma he never knew what to expect. She always surprised him with amazing behavior. One time, he watched her playing a game of catch with a piece of sea-weed. She plucked a golden-colored frond of kelp from the bottom, then swam up near the surface and let it go. As the kelp drifted lazily toward the bottom, Wilma swam down and caught it on her head. Then she swam back toward the surface and did it all over again.

One time, Wilma really helped Jim. He had accidentally dropped his car keys over the side of his boat. As he was getting ready to put on his SCUBA gear to go looking for them, Wilma popped up with the keys in her mouth! She was a true friend indeed.

Wilma and Jim spent much of their time swimming around "mom," Wilma's bright red buoy. After playing or exploring, Jim and Wilma would rest on the surface near the buoy. Sometimes, he would float quietly and Wilma would move in close. She often reminded him of a dog snuggling on a couch. She liked having the top of her head scratched. As Jim petted her lovingly, Wilma would go into a kind of trance. He loved to watch as her eyes slowly closed.

Whenever Jim climbed out of the water, Wilma was always nearby. She loved to rub alongside his boat's smooth, rubber pontoons. Sometimes, she even took Jim's hand in her mouth, gently tugging at him. It was as if she did not want Jim to leave. Jim knew that beluga whales are very social animals. In the wild, they spend most of their time with other belugas. They are rarely alone. Jim could see that Wilma was lonely.

On a few occasions, Jim had seen Wilma swimming with seals in the bay. She had even been seen frolicking with pilot whales that passed through the area in the summer. In winter, when fewer people were around, Wilma found company among the divers that worked harvesting sea urchins in the bay.

It was not long before the story of Wilma had been told far and wide. A few local people began bringing tourists to see the friendly, white whale. She had become quite a celebrity. People came in boats, canoes, and kayaks to see if the stories they had heard were really true.

Of all her visitors, Wilma seemed to love children the most. A few times, children even went into the water with her. Wearing life jackets, they floated on the surface, waiting for the whale to approach. Wilma allowed them to touch her head and stroke her sides. Sometimes, she would come face to face with a child and would look right into the child's eyes.

Several years passed and Wilma was still at home in Chedabucto Bay. Summers cooled into falls, winters melted into springs, and the little, white whale went about her daily routine. By this time, Wilma's "smiling" face had charmed many people.

Early one spring morning, Jim Johnson loaded his SCUBA gear into his boat. Then he motored out to the big red buoy in the middle of the bay. He looked in all directions, but he could not see Wilma anywhere on the surface. He steered his boat around the bay, but still, he could not find her.

Back at the buoy, Jim put on his diving gear and dove into the water. He followed the rusty anchor chain down to the bay's sandy bottom. He squinted as he peered carefully through the murky green water. He swam to the rocky beach, picked up two stones, and banged them together as he had done so many times before. But this time, his "underwater telegraph" did not work. Wilma was nowhere to be found.

Jim went back to his boat and sailed Chedabucto Bay looking for signs of his friend. He saw nothing. He returned again the next day, and the day after that. There were no signs of Wilma anywhere. In the months that followed, Jim checked the bay occasionally. In his heart, however, he knew Wilma was gone.

Jim was saddened, but he knew Wilma's departure was for the best. He treasured the special friendship he had with her, but he also understood that she was a wild animal. He knew she must be free to roam the sea. Wilma needed to find other beluga whales and maybe even start a family of her own. Jim had always known that he could not hold on to Wilma forever. She had come to his pretty, little bay on her own and she had left on her own—the way it should be.

Jim's dream of swimming with a whale had
come true beyond his wildest imagination.
His memories of Wilma would last him a
lifetime. He hoped that somewhere
out in the sea she was having new
adventures with other whales.
Secretly, he even hoped that
maybe she was telling them
the stories of her life among
the humans—wonderful
stories of when she was
a whale on her own.

Words to Know

Buoy a floating marker in an ocean or river.

Cautiously carefully.

Frolicking happily playing.

Frond a large, divided leaf on a stalk of a plant or tree.

Kelp a brown, edible seaweed.

Orphan juvenile whose parents are dead.

Osprey a large, fish-eating hawk.

Pod a group of whales or dolphins that live and travel together.

Pontoon part on the bottom of some boats that help them float.

Sonar an instrument that uses sound waves to measure the depth of water, or to find the location of underwater objects.

Sound wave a series of vibrations that can be heard in air, liquid, or solids.

Technique a certain way of doing something.

Telegraph a device or system for sending messages.

For More Information

Books

Facklam, Marjorie. Pamela Johnson (Illustrator). *Bees Dance and Whales Sing: The Mysteries of Animal Communication*. San Francisco, CA: Sierra Club Juveniles, 1992.

Funston, Sylvia. Olena Kassian (Illustrator). *St. Lawrence Beluga* (Endangered Animals). Toronto, CN: Owl Communications, 1992.

Kelsey, Elin. *Finding Out About Whales*. Toronto, CN: Owl Communications, 1998.

Prevost, John F. *Beluga Whales* (Whales). Minneapolis, MN: Abdo Publishing Company, 1996.

Web Sites

AquaFacts
Find answers to all your whale questions—**oceanlink.island.net/ aquafacts/Beluga2.html**

Beluga Whales
Learn more about beluga habitat, senses, characteristics, and reproduction— **www.seaworld.org/ beluga_whales/beFirst.html**

National Aquarium in Baltimore
Find out why belugas are called "sea canaries," as well as why and where they migrate—**www.aqua.org/ animals/species/beluga.html**